Nature Upclose

A Ladybug's Life

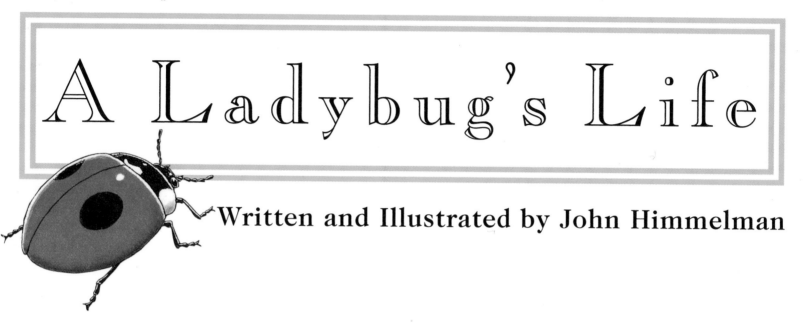

Written and Illustrated by John Himmelman

Children's Press®
A Division of Grolier Publishing

New York London Hong Kong Sydney
Danbury, Connecticut

For Kay Kudlinski, a fellow writer, artist, and observer of things that scurry, crawl, swim, and fly.

Library of Congress Cataloging-in-Publication Data

Himmelman, John
   A ladybug's life / written and illustrated by John Himmelman
      p.   cm. — (Nature upclose)
   Summary: Illustrations and simple text follow the daily activities of a ladybug through its life cycle, from summer to fall.
   ISBN 0-516-26353-6
   1. Ladybugs—Juvenile literature.   2. Ladybugs—Life cycles—Juvenile literatutue.   [1. Ladybugs.]   I. Title.   II. Series: Himmelman, John.   Nature upclose.
QL596.C65H56   1998
595.76'9—dc21
                                                            97-9129
                                                               CIP
                                                                AC

Two-spotted Ladybug
Adalia bipunctata

There are more than 5,000 different kinds of ladybugs in the world. The two-spotted ladybug is common throughout North America. It usually lives in fields, meadows, and gardens. Ladybugs may lay eggs several times in a single year. Sometimes, they spend the winter in the windowsills of homes.

Ladybugs are very helpful to humans. Both the larvae and adults feed on aphids and other small insects that destroy our crops and gardens. Ladybugs were so well liked by the Europeans who lived about 600 years ago that they were originally called "Beetles of Our Lady." (Our Lady was the Virgin Mary.) This name was later shortened to "ladybug."

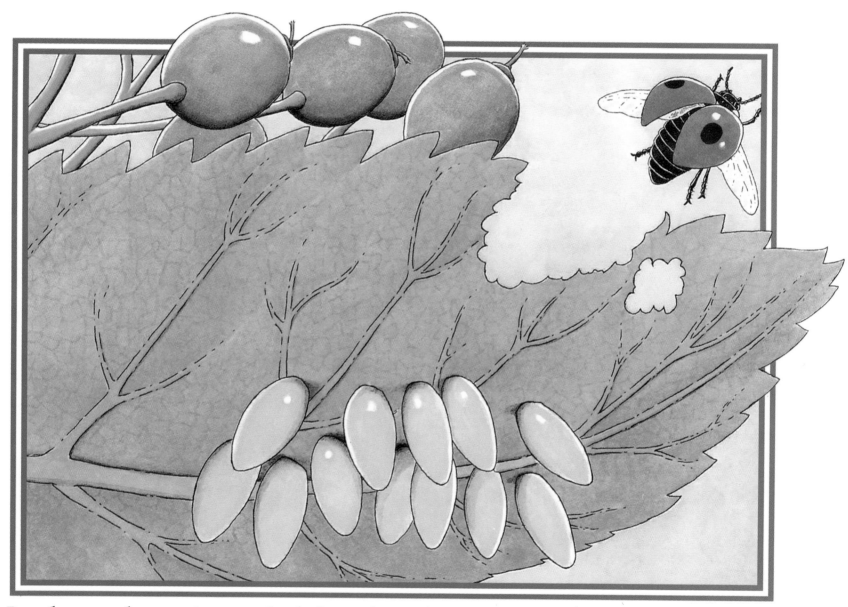

In the early spring, a ladybug lays her eggs on a leaf.

Soon, a ladybug *larva* squeezes out of her egg.

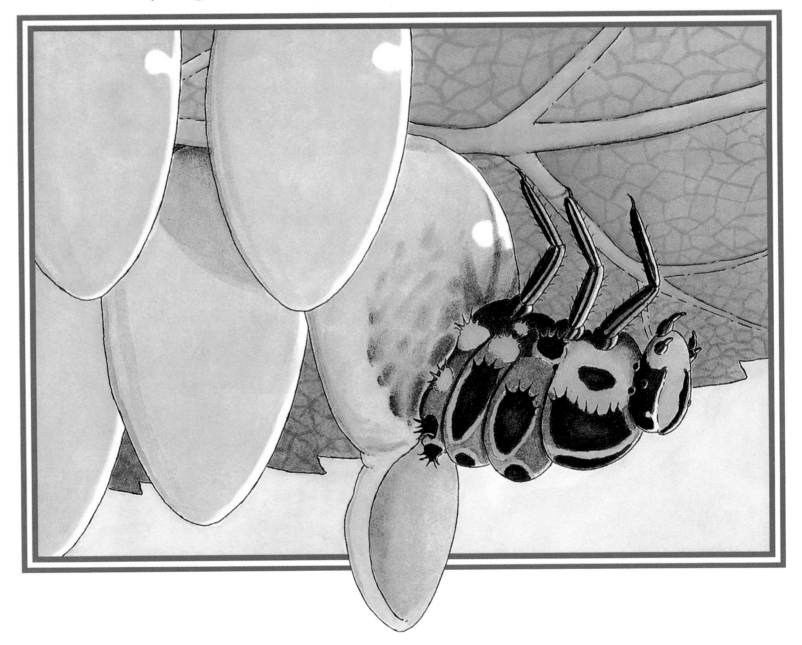

Good morning, spring.

The ladybug larva plucks an *aphid* off a rose stem.

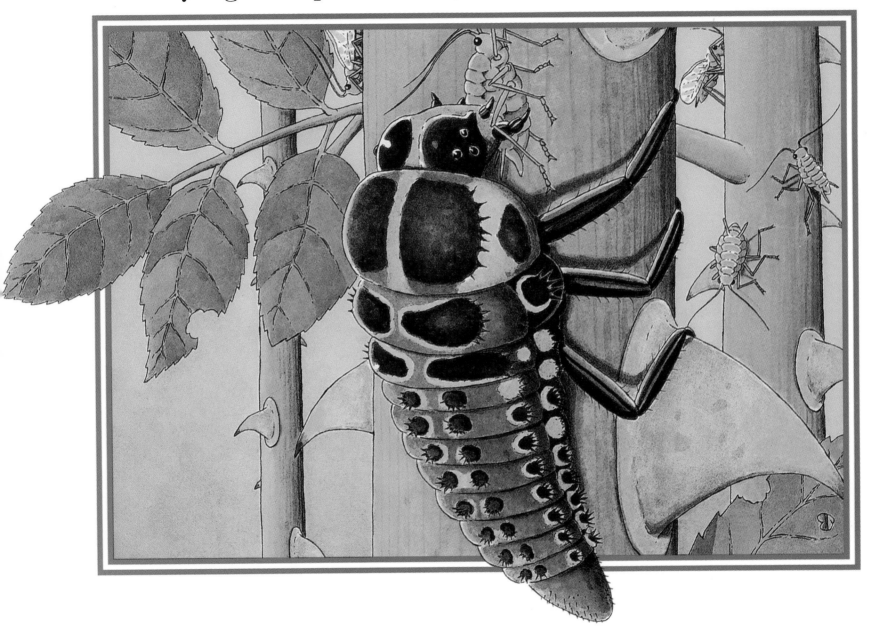

She grows bigger and bigger each day.

Soon the ladybug larva changes into a ladybug *pupa*.

Then, the ladybug pupa changes into a ladybug beetle.

Good morning, summer.

The ladybug beetle searches for food.

Mealybugs make a good meal.

The ladybug beetle climbs to the top of an aster.

And then flies off through the air.

A *warbler* tries to catch the ladybug beetle.

She gets away. But a *robberfly* is not as lucky.

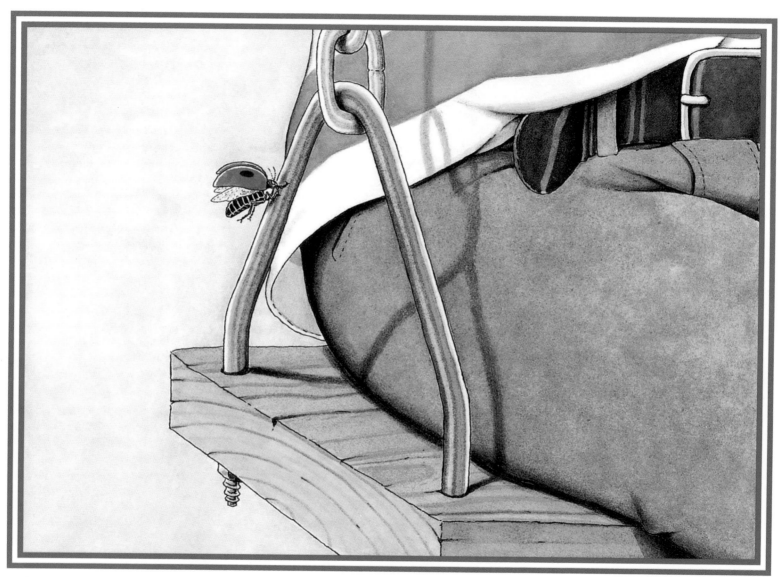

The ladybug beetle lands on a child's swing.

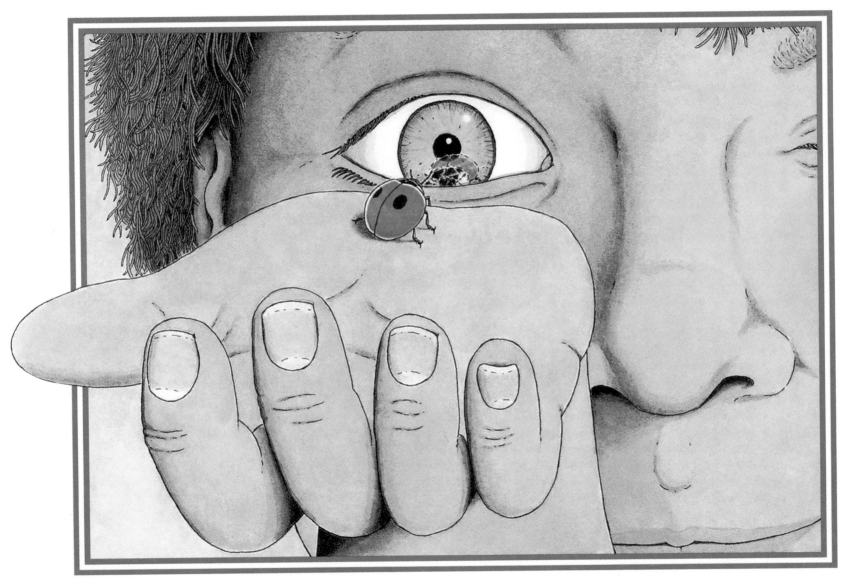

She looks in the child's eye.

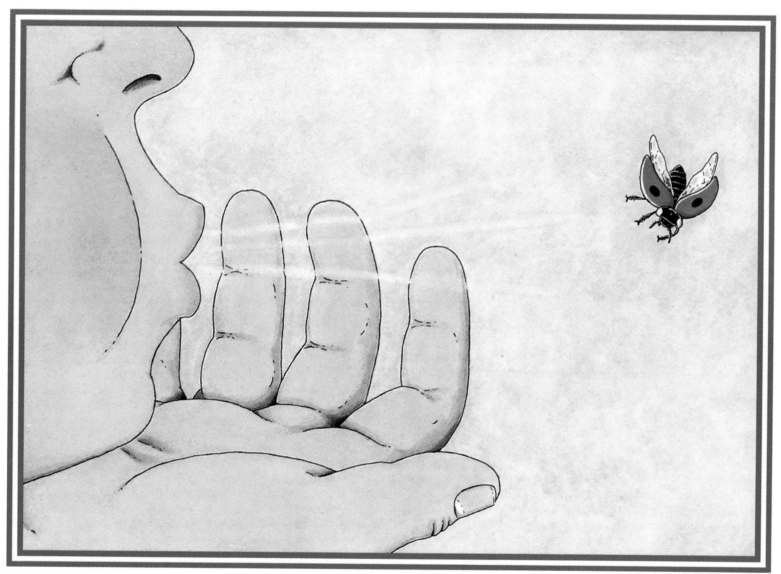

"Ladybug, ladybug, fly away," says the child.

The ladybug beetle lands on a wild rose.

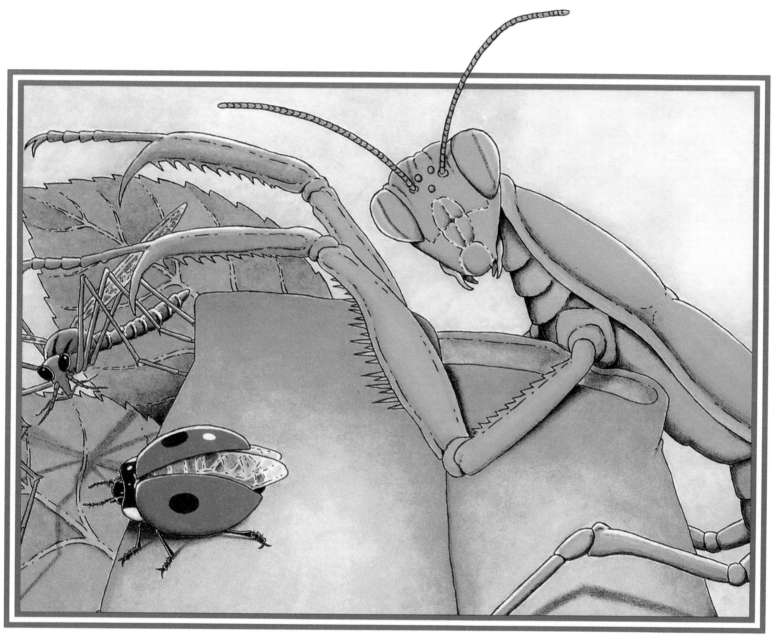

But a *praying mantis* is waiting.

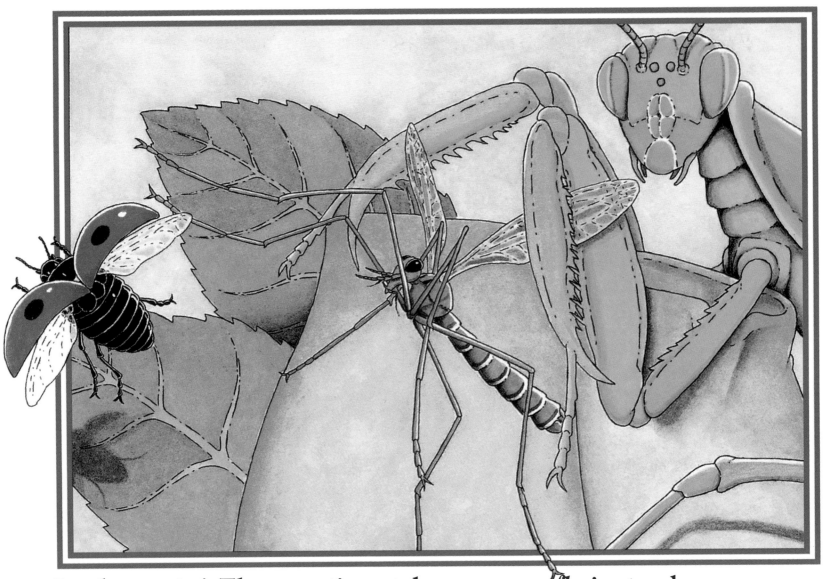

Lucky again! The mantis catches a *cranefly* instead.

It is time to find a male ladybug beetle.

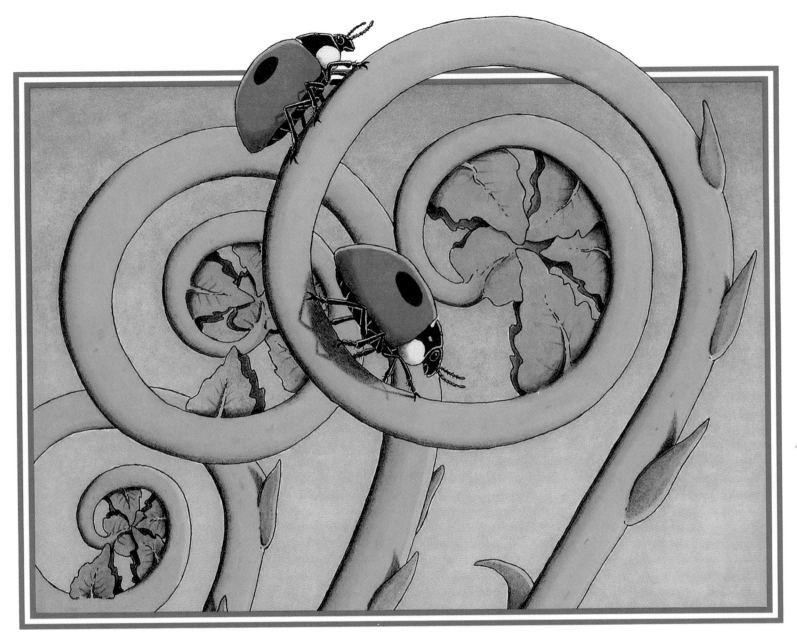

She searches and snoops. She seeks and hunts.

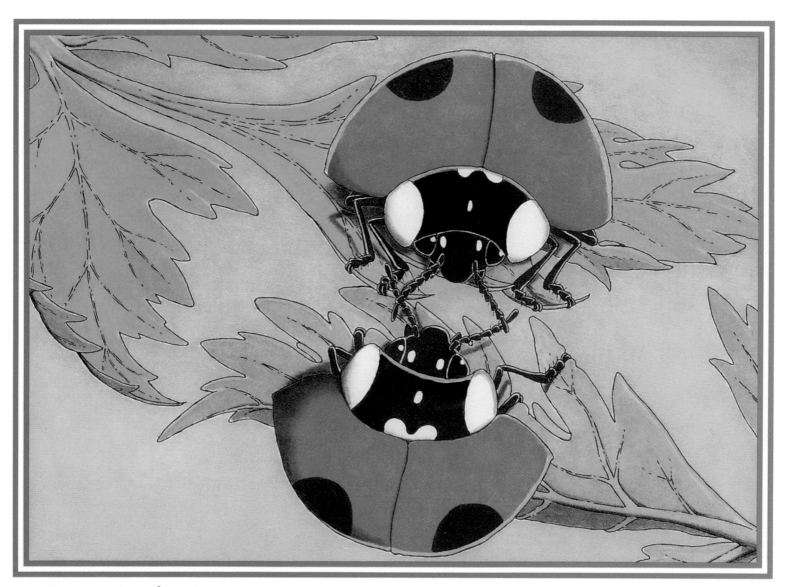

At last, she finds a mate.

Now the ladybug beetle lays eggs of her own.

When summer has passed, the autumn leaves fall.

As it grows cold, the ladybug beetle grows sleepy.

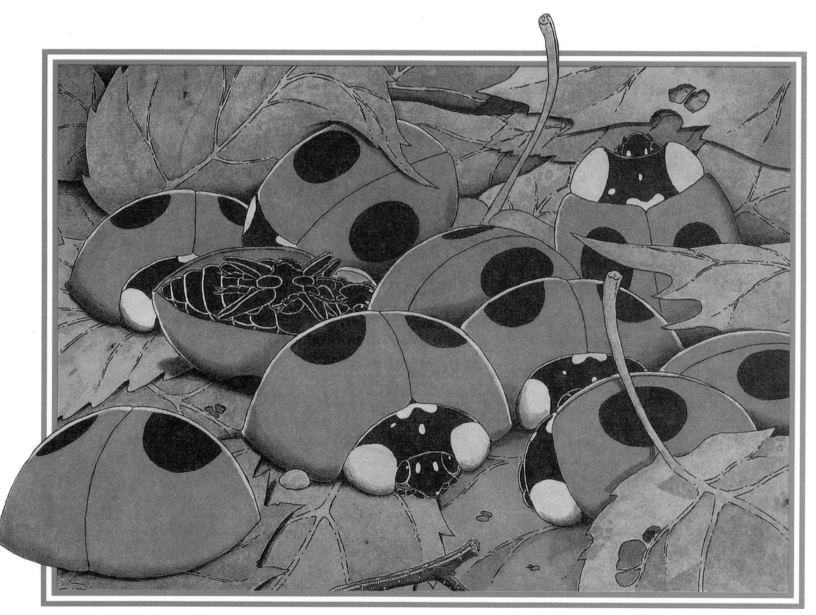

She sleeps through winter with her ladybug friends.

Goodnight, until spring, ladybug beetle.

Words You Know

aphid—a tiny green insect that eats roses and other plants.

cranefly—a long-legged insect that looks like a large mosquito.

larva—the first stage of an insect's life.

mealybug—a small, round insect that destroys fruit trees.

praying mantis—a large, green insect that eats other insects.

pupa—the second stage of an insect's life.

robberfly—an insect that hunts flies.

warbler—a small songbird.

About the Author

John Himmelman has written or illustrated more than forty books for children, including *Ibis: A True Whale Story*, *Wanted: Perfect Parents*, and *J.J. Versus the Babysitter*. His books have received honors such as Pick of the List, Book of the Month, JLG Selection, and the ABC Award. He is also a naturalist who enjoys turning over dead logs, crawling through grass, kneeling over puddles, and gazing at the sky. His greatest joy is sharing these experiences with others. John lives in Killingworth, Connecticut, with his wife Betsy who is an art teacher. They have two children, Jeff and Liz.